Science Words
Digging for Fossils

Name

Date

To parents
Starting on this page, your child will be introduced to reading and writing important words used in science. The pictures will help your child understand the meaning of each word.

■ Trace the letters while saying each word.

W9-BUV-079

■ Trace the letters while saying each word.

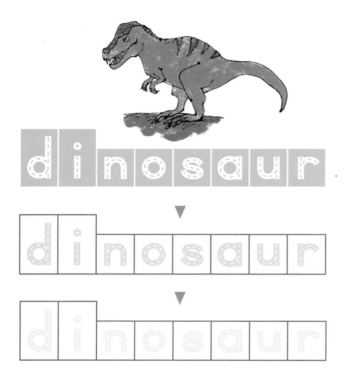

d i n o s a u r .

▼

d i n o s a u r

▼

d i n o s a u r

f o s s i l

▼

f o s s i l

▼

f o s s i l

s h e l l s

▼

s h e l l s

▼

s h e l l s

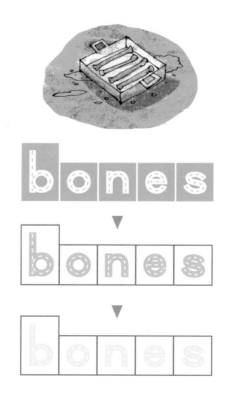

b o n e s

▼

b o n e s

▼

b o n e s

Science Words
Digging for Fossils

■ Trace the letters while saying each word.

dinosaur

▼

dinosaur

▼

dinosaur

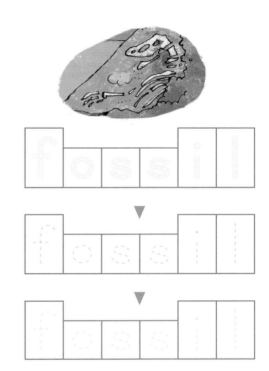

fossil

▼

fossil

▼

fossil

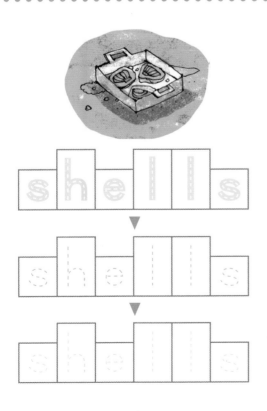

shells

▼

shells

▼

shells

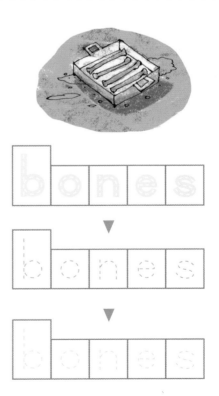

bones

▼

bones

▼

bones

■ Trace and write the letters while saying each word.

d i n o s a u r

▼

d i
n o s a u r

▼

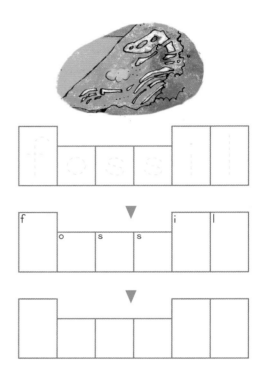

f o s s i l

▼

f o s s i l

▼

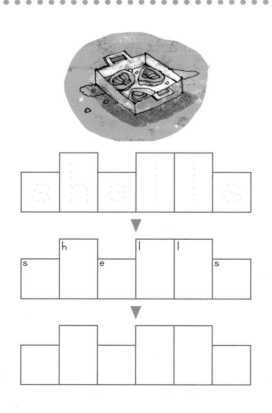

s h e l l s

▼

h l l
s e s

▼

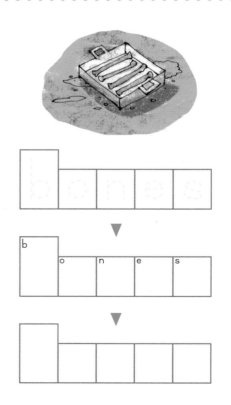

b o n e s

▼

b
o n e s

▼

Science Words
Simple Machines

Name

Date

To parents
Your child may need your help reading each word aloud at first. This book provides plenty of practice and repetition, so your child can eventually learn to read each word on his or her own.

■ Trace the letters while saying each word.

■ Trace the letters while saying each word.

pulley

pulley

pulley

wedge

wedge

wedge

lever

lever

lever

screw

screw

screw

Science Words
Simple Machines

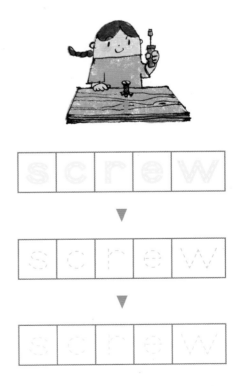
Name

Date

■ Trace the letters while saying each word.

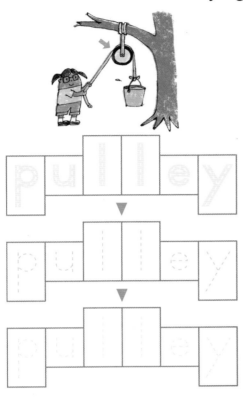

pulley
▼
pulley
▼
pulley

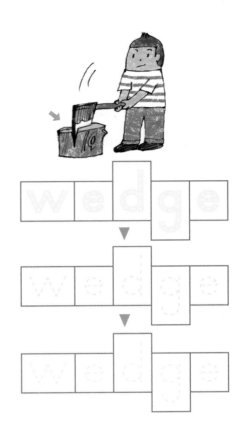

wedge
▼
wedge
▼
wedge

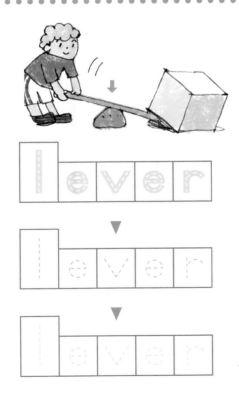

lever
▼
lever
▼
lever

screw
▼
screw
▼
screw

■ Trace and write the letters while saying each word.

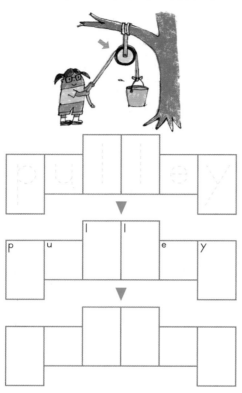

p u l l e y

▼

p u l l e y

▼

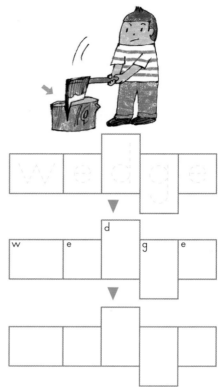

w e d g e

▼

w e d g e

▼

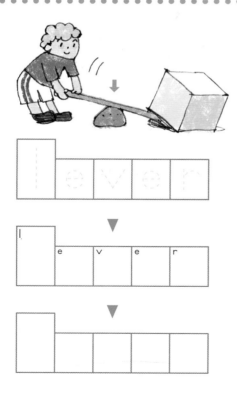

l e v e r

▼

l e v e r

▼

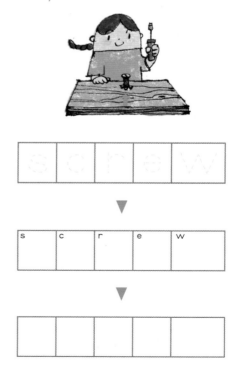

s c r e w

▼

s c r e w

▼

Science Words

States of Matter

Name

Date

■ Trace the letters while saying each word.

solids

liquids

gases

matter

9

■ Trace the letters while saying each word.

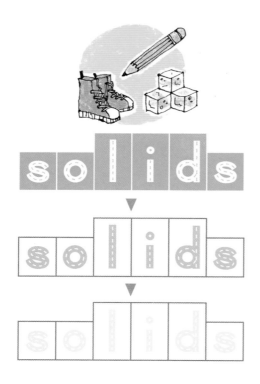

solids

solids

solids

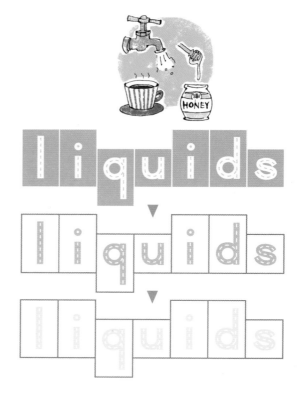

liquids

liquids

liquids

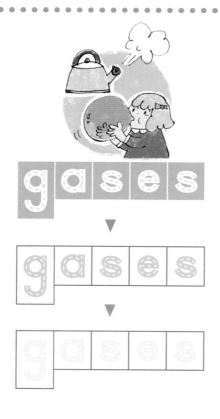

gases

gases

gases

matter

matter

matter

6 Science Words
States of Matter

Name

Date

■ Trace the letters while saying each word.

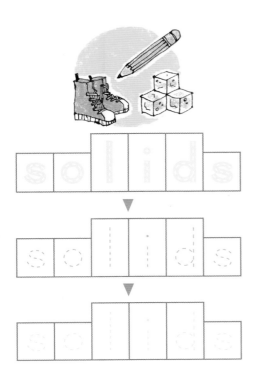

solids

solids

solids

liquids

liquids

liquids

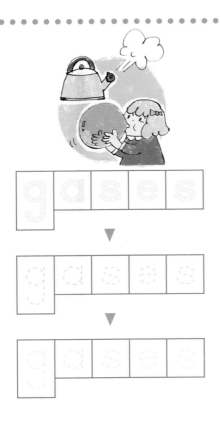

gases

gases

gases

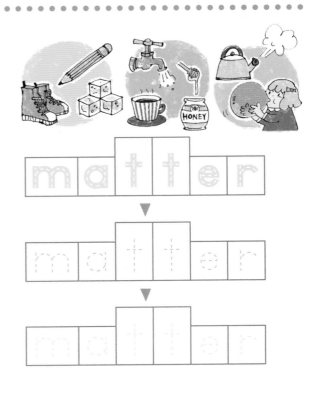

matter

matter

matter

■ Trace and write the letters while saying each word.

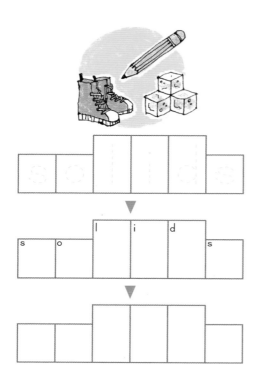

s	o	l	i	d	s

▼

s	o	l	i	d		s

▼

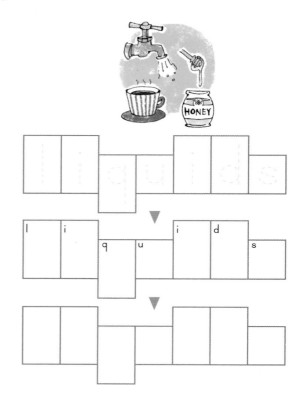

l	i	q	u	i	d	s

▼

| l | i | | q | u | | i | d | | s |

▼

g	a	s	e	s

▼

g	a	s	e	s

▼

m	a	t	t	e	r

▼

m	a	t	t	e	r

▼

12

Science Words

Ladybug Life Cycle

■ Trace the letters while saying each word.

adult

pupa

eggs

larva

■ Trace the letters while saying each word.

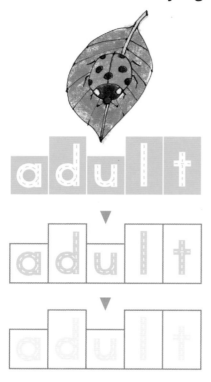

adult

adult

adult

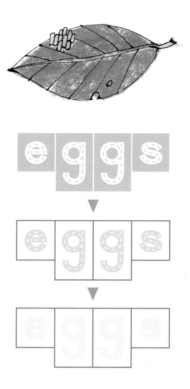

eggs

eggs

eggs

larva

larva

larva

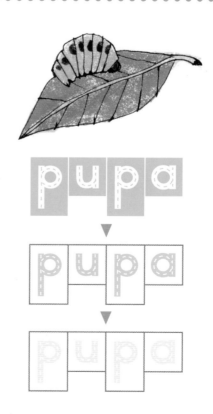

pupa

pupa

pupa

8 Science Words
Ladybug Life Cycle

■ Trace the letters while saying each word.

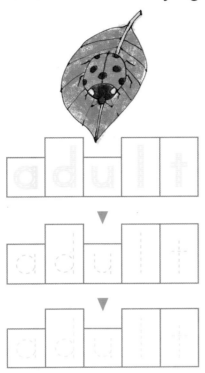

adult

▼

adult

▼

adult

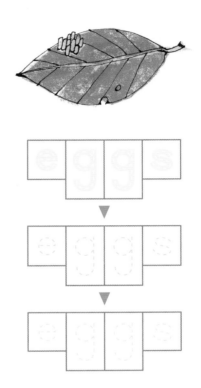

eggs

▼

eggs

▼

eggs

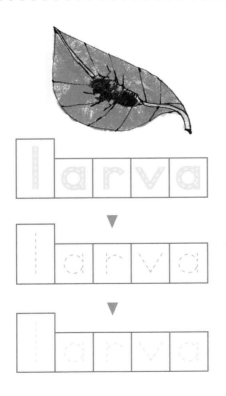

larva

▼

larva

▼

larva

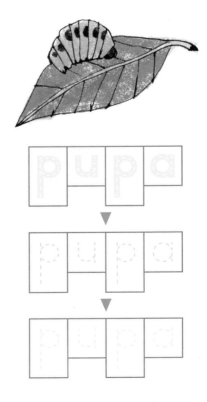

pupa

▼

pupa

▼

pupa

■ Trace and write the letters while saying each word.

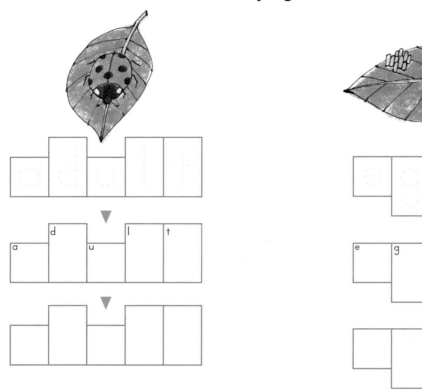

| a | d | u | l | t |

| e | g | g | s |

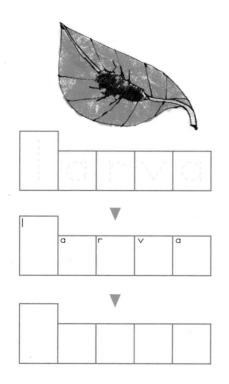

| l | a | r | v | a |

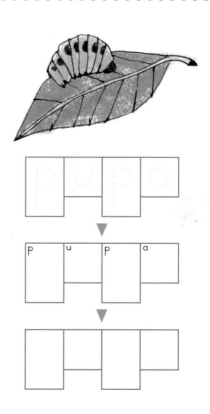

| p | u | p | a |

9 Science Words
Review

Name _____

Date _____

■ Write the letters while saying each word.

| d | i | n | o | s | a | u | r |

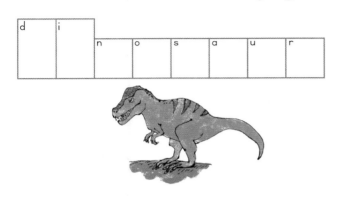

| f | o | s | s | i | l |

| s | h | e | l | l | s |

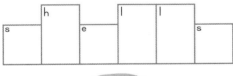

| b | o | n | e | s |

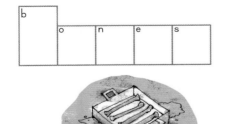

| p | u | l | l | e | y |

| w | e | d | g | e |

| l | e | v | e | r |

| s | c | r | e | w |

17

■ Write the letters while saying each word.

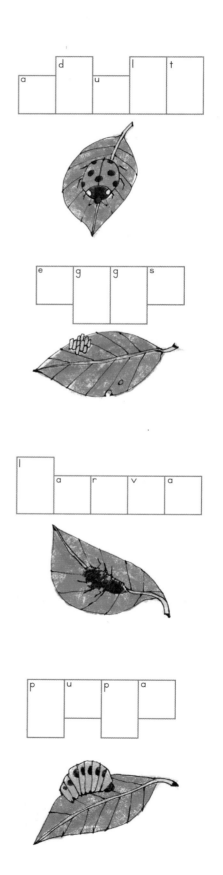

Math Words
Measurement

Name

Date

To parents
Starting on this page, your child will be introduced to reading and writing important words used in math. The pictures will help your child understand the meaning of each word.

■ Trace the letters while saying each word.

gram

kilogram

liter

meter

■ Trace the letters while saying each word.

gram
▼
gram
▼
gram

kilogram
▼
kilogram
▼
kilogram

liter
▼
liter
▼
liter

meter
▼
meter
▼
meter

Name

Date

■ Trace the letters while saying each word.

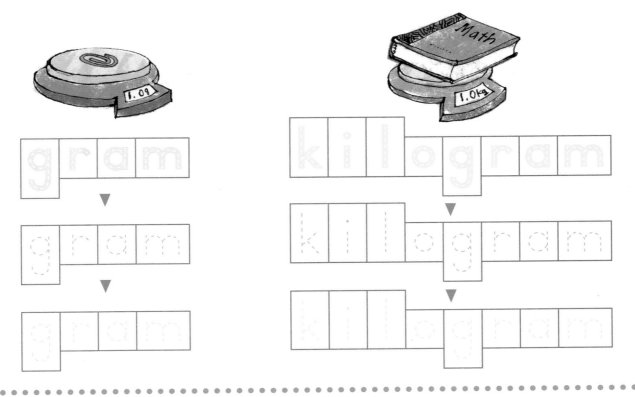

gram

gram

gram

kilogram

kilogram

kilogram

liter

liter

liter

meter

meter

meter

■ Trace and write the letters while saying each word.

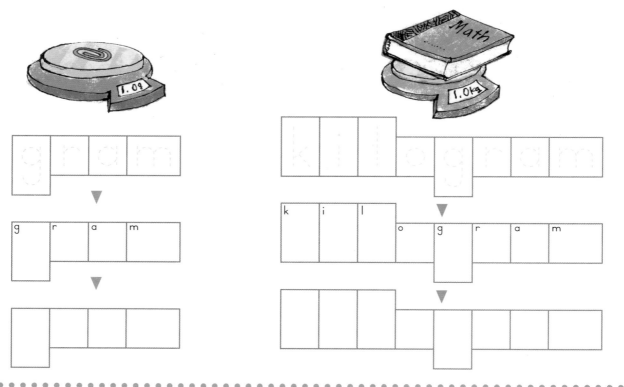

Name

Date

■ Trace the letters while saying each word.

symbols   table

graphs diagrams

■ Trace the letters while saying each word.

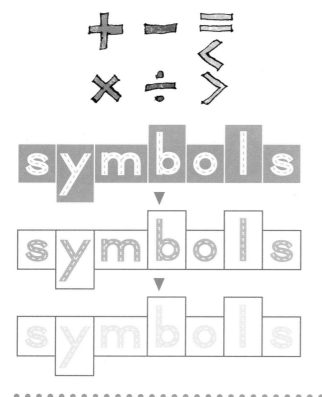

symbols

symbols

symbols

teacher	Number of students
Ms. Curley	23
Mr. Liu	21
Ms. Nunez	19
Mrs. Williams	22

table

table

table

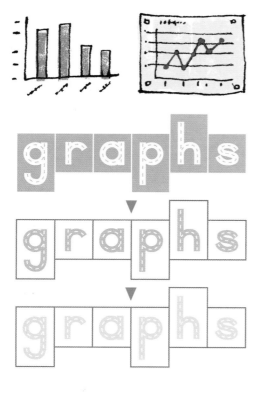

graphs

graphs

graphs

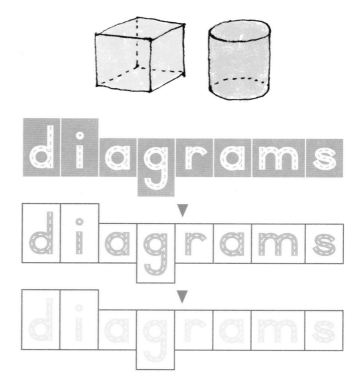

diagrams

diagrams

diagrams

Math Words
Communicating Math

Name

Date

■ Trace the letters while saying each word.

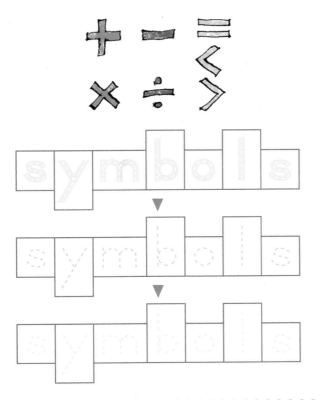

symbols

symbols

symbols

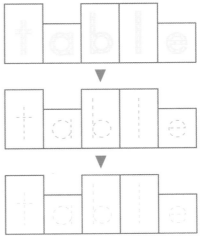

table

table

table

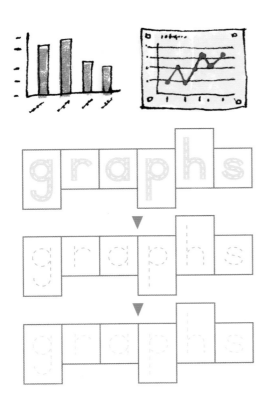

graphs

graphs

graphs

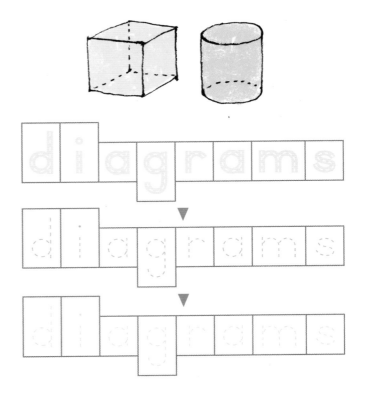

diagrams

diagrams

diagrams

■ Trace and write the letters while saying each word.

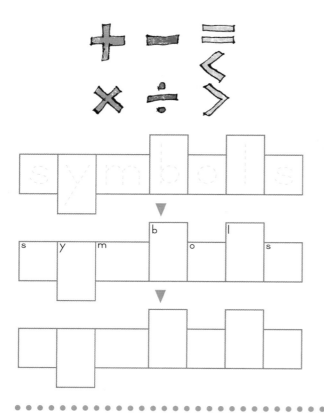

teacher	Number of students
Ms. Curley	23
Mr. Liu	21
Ms. Nunez	19
Mrs. Williams	22

symbols

table

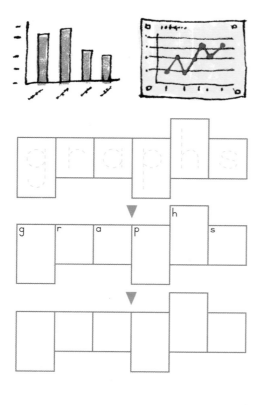

graphs

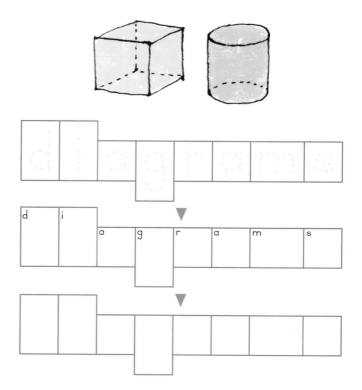

diagrams

26

Math Words

Understanding Multiplication

Name

Date

■ Trace the letters while saying each word.

factors   product

$3 \times 4 = 12$

row

column

■ Trace the letters while saying each word.

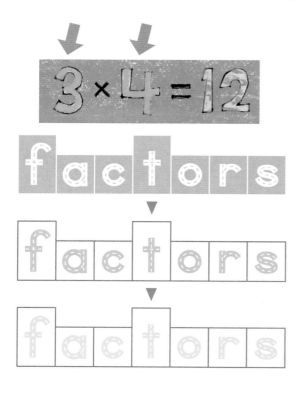

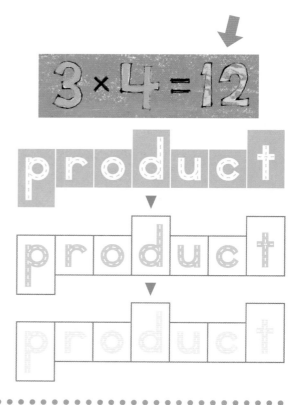

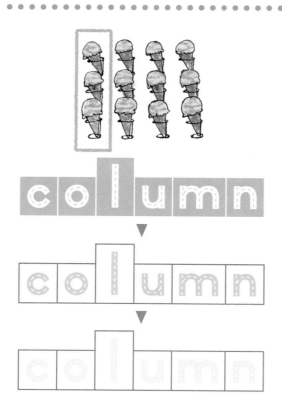

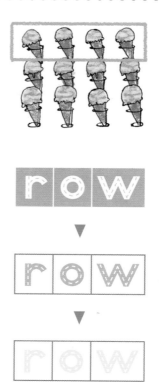

28

Math Words

Understanding Multiplication

Name

Date

■ Trace the letters while saying each word.

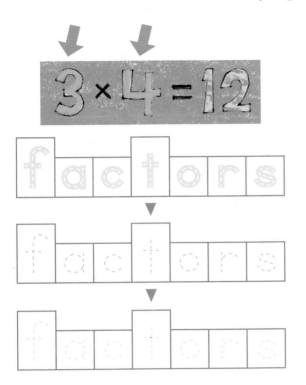

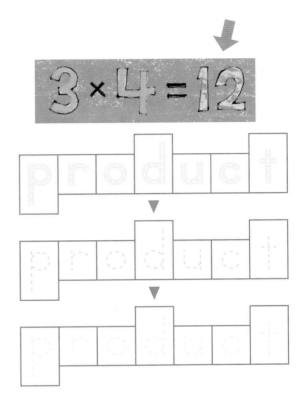

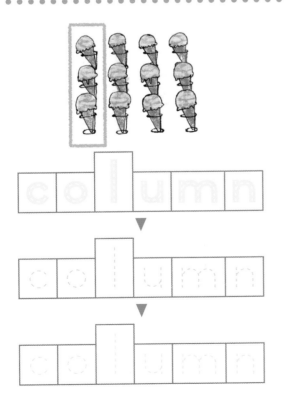

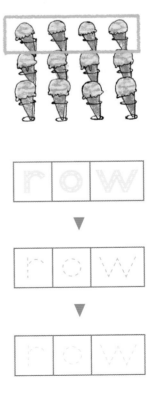

■ Trace and write the letters while saying each word.

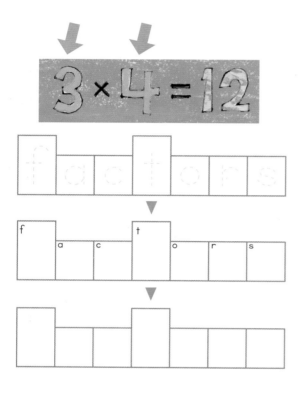

f a c t o r s

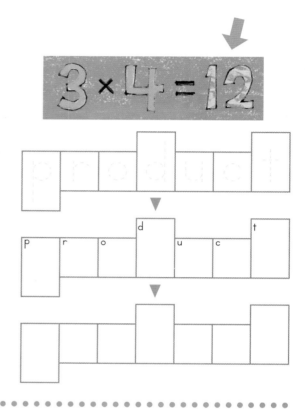

p r o d u c t

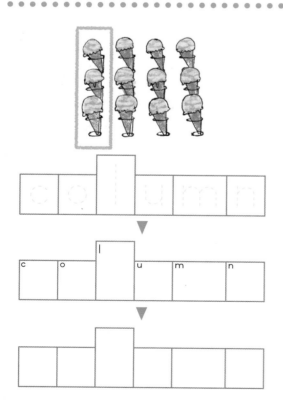

c o l u m n

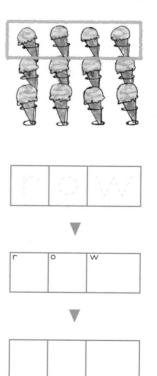

r o w

Math Words
Geometry

■ Trace the letters while saying each word.

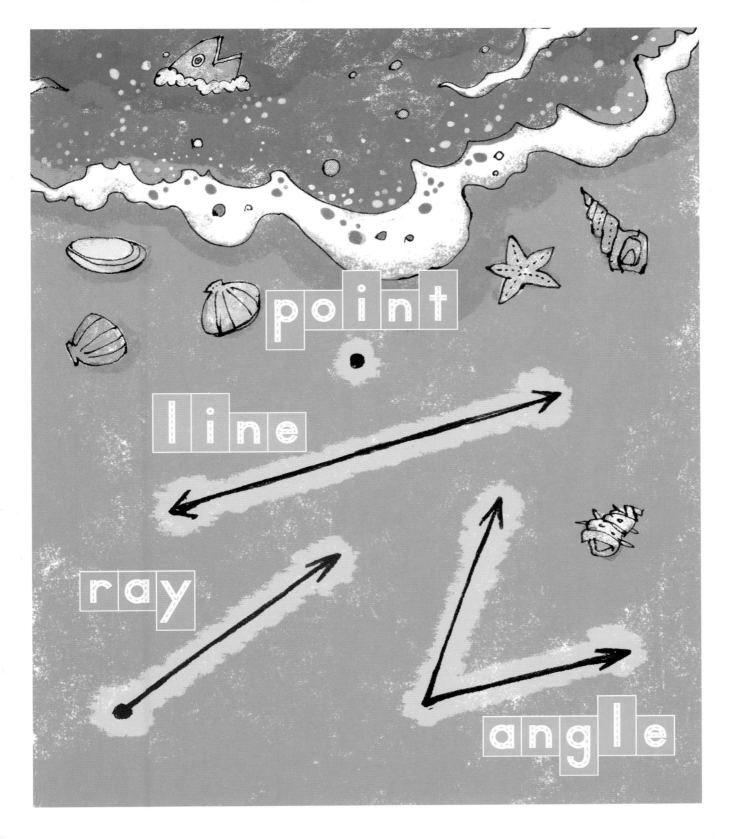

■ Trace the letters while saying each word.

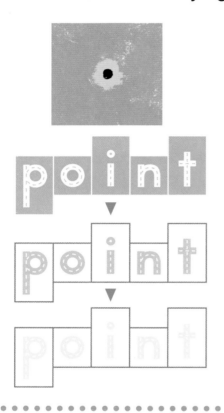

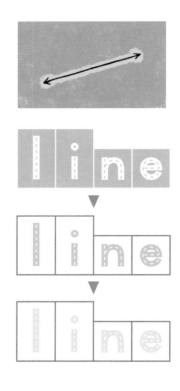

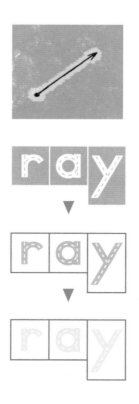

Name

Date

■ Trace the letters while saying each word.

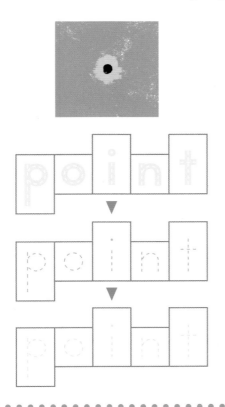

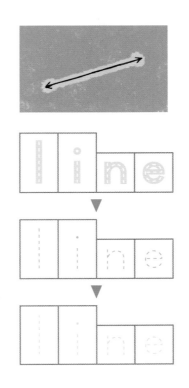

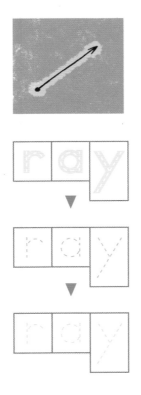

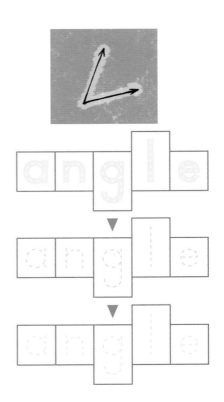

33

■ Trace and write the letters while saying each word.

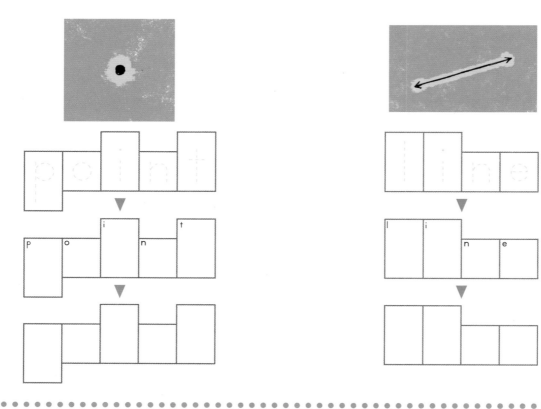

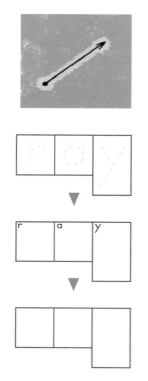

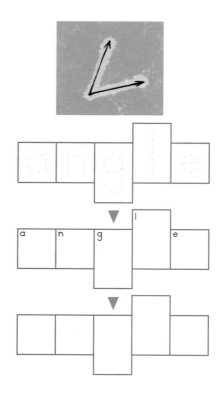

Name

Date

■ Write the letters while saying each word.

g | r | a | m

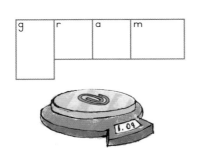

s | y | m | b | o | l | s

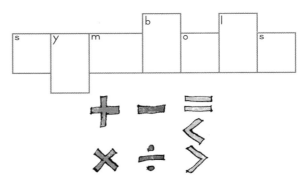

k | i | l | o | g | r | a | m

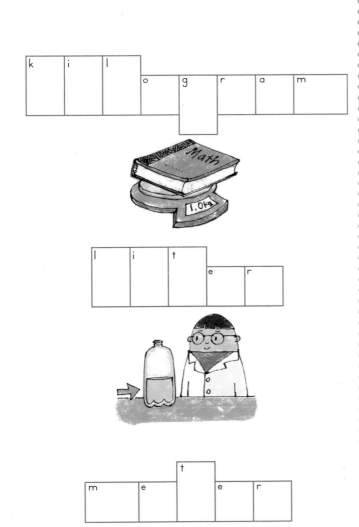

t | a | b | l | e

teacher	Number of students
Ms. Curley	23
Mr. Liu	21
Ms. Nunez	19
Mrs. Williams	22

l | i | t | e | r

g | r | a | p | h | s

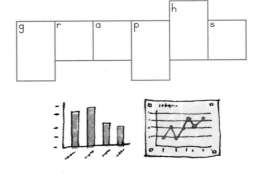

m | e | t | e | r

d | i | a | g | r | a | m | s

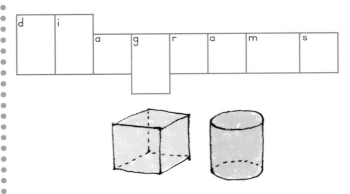

■ Write the letters while saying each word.

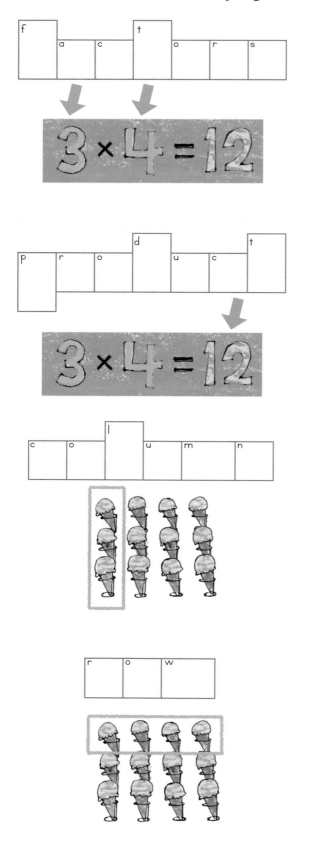

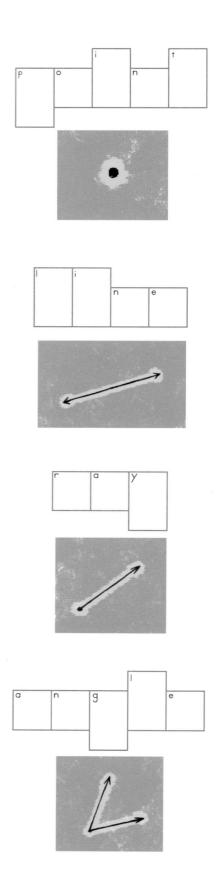

Social Studies Words
Using a Globe

Name

Date

To parents
Starting on this page, your child will be introduced to reading and writing important words used in social studies. The pictures will help your child understand the meaning of each word.

■ Trace the letters while saying each word.

■ Trace the letters while saying each word.

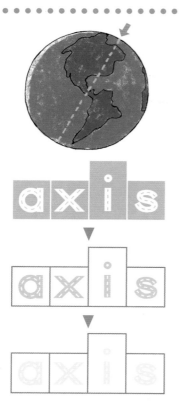

Social Studies Words
Using a Globe

Name

Date

■ Trace the letters while saying each word.

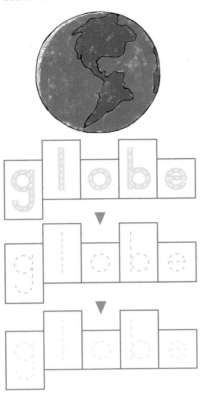

globe

globe

globe

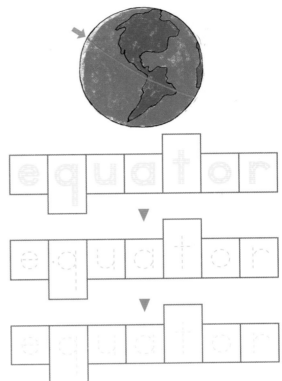

equator

equator

equator

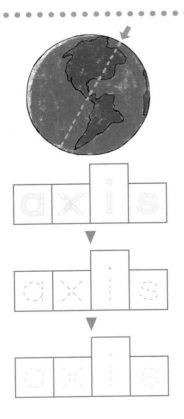

axis

axis

axis

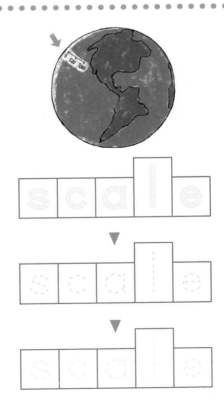

scale

scale

scale

■ Trace and write the letters while saying each word.

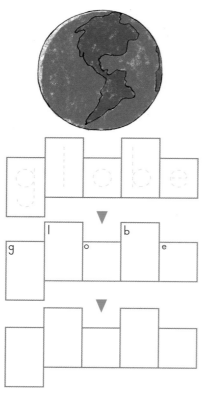

g l o b e

g l o b e

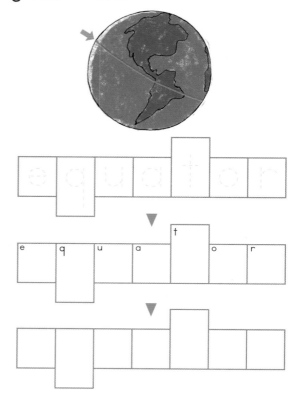

e q u a t o r

e q u a t o r

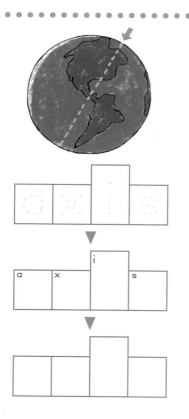

a x i s

a x i s

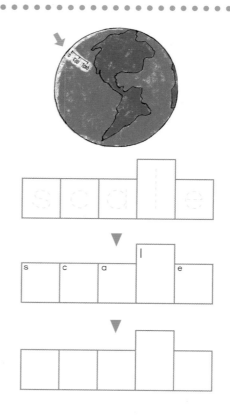

s c a l e

s c a l e

Name

Date

■ Trace the letters while saying each word.

urban

rural

local

global

■ Trace the letters while saying each word.

urban
▼
urban
▼
urban

rural
▼
rural
▼
rural

local
▼
local
▼
local

global
▼
global
▼
global

Social Studies Words

Kinds of Communities

Name

Date

■ Trace the letters while saying each word.

urban

▼

urban

▼

urban

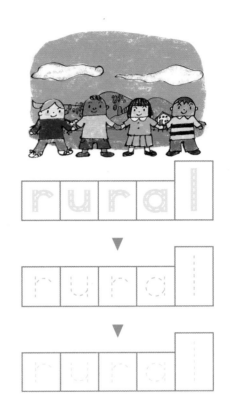

rural

▼

rural

▼

rural

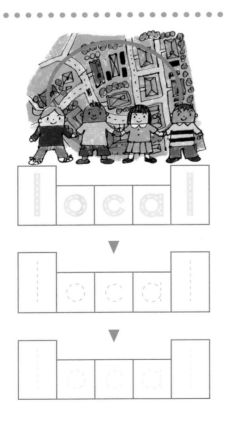

local

▼

local

▼

local

global

▼

global

▼

global

■ Trace and write the letters while saying each word.

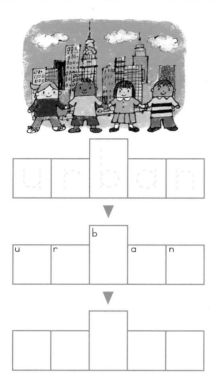

u r b a n

▼

b
u r a n

▼

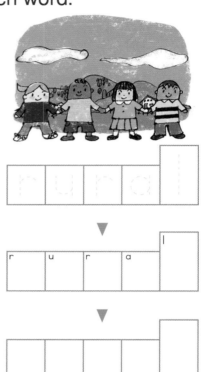

r u r a l

▼

l
r u r a

▼

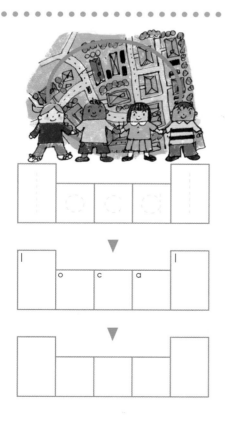

l o c a l

▼

l l
o c a

▼

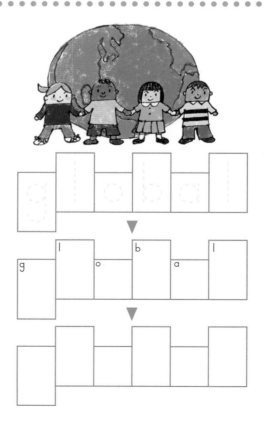

g l o b a l

▼

l b l
g o a

▼

Social Studies Words
Economics

Name

Date

■ Trace the letters while saying each word.

demand

supply

scarcity

surplus

■ Trace the letters while saying each word.

demand

▼

demand

▼

demand

supply

▼

supply

▼

supply

scarcity

▼

scarcity

▼

scarcity

surplus

▼

surplus

▼

surplus

Social Studies Words
Economics

Name

Date

■ Trace the letters while saying each word.

demand

▼

demand

▼

demand

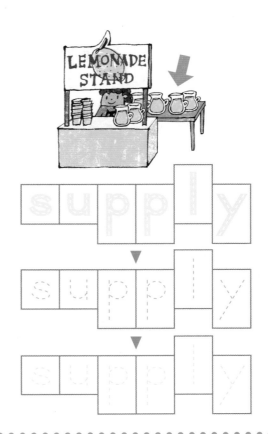

supply

▼

supply

▼

supply

scarcity

▼

scarcity

▼

scarcity

surplus

▼

surplus

▼

surplus

■ Trace and write the letters while saying each word.

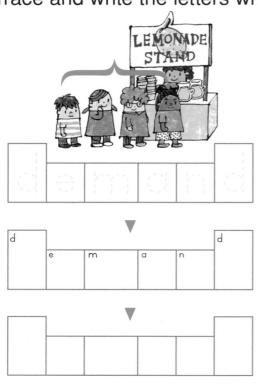

d e m a n d

▼

| d | | | | | d |
| | e | m | | a | n | |

▼

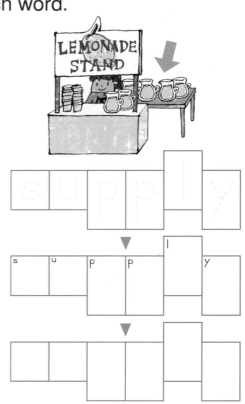

s u p p l y

▼

| s | u | p | p | l | | y |

▼

s c a r c i t y

▼

| s | c | a | r | c | i | t | y |

▼

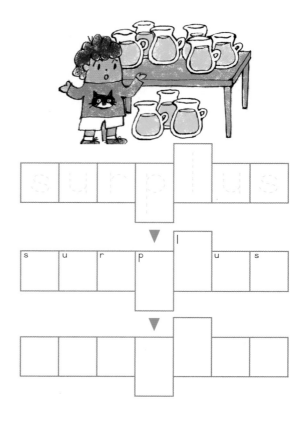

s u r p l u s

▼

| s | u | r | p | l | u | s |

▼

Name

Date

■ Trace the letters while saying each word.

campaign

debate

ballot

voting

■ Trace the letters while saying each word.

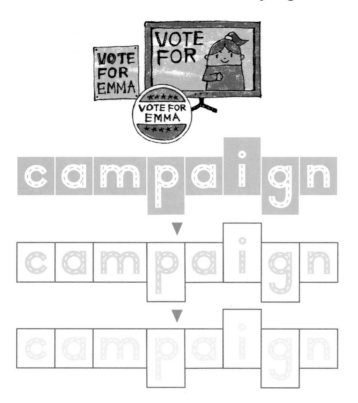

campaign

campaign

campaign

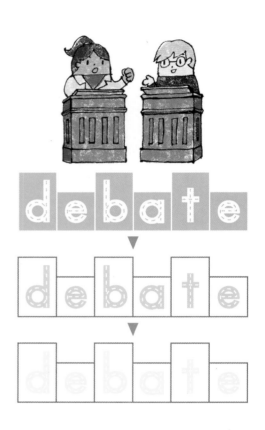

debate

debate

debate

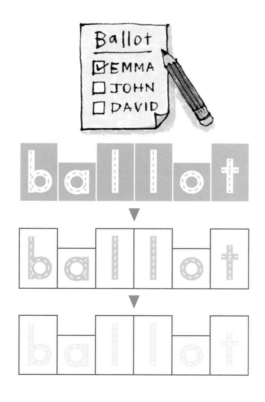

ballot

ballot

ballot

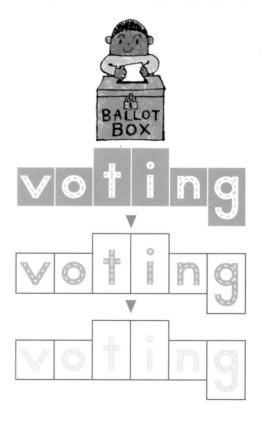

voting

voting

voting

Social Studies Words

Elections

■ Trace the letters while saying each word.

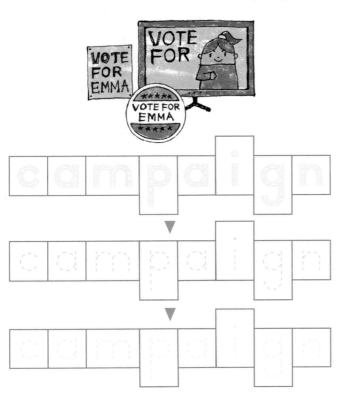

campaign

campaign

campaign

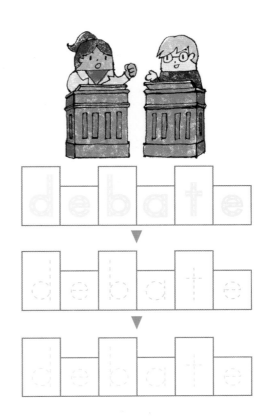

debate

debate

debate

ballot

ballot

ballot

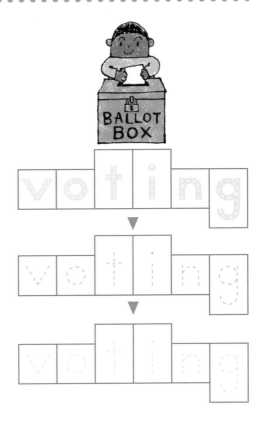

voting

voting

voting

■ Trace and write the letters while saying each word.

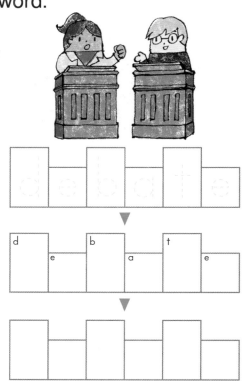

c | a | m | p | a | i | g | n

d | e | b | a | t | e

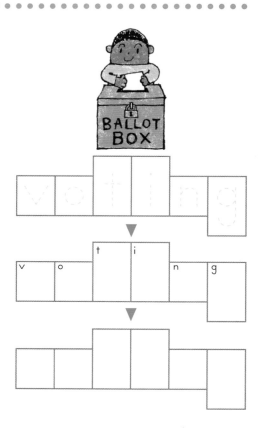

b | a | l | l | o | t

v | o | t | i | n | g

Social Studies Words

Review

Name

Date

■ Write the letters while saying each word.

g | l | | o | b | e

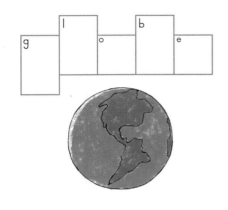

e | q | u | a | t | o | r

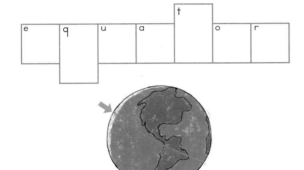

a | x | i | s

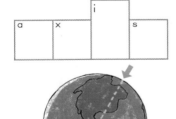

s | c | a | l | e

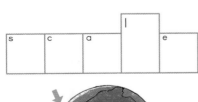

u | r | b | a | n

r | u | r | a | l

l | o | c | a | l

g | l | o | b | a | l

■ Write the letters while saying each word.

d e m a n d

s u p p l y

s c a r c i t y

s u r p l u s

c a m p a i g n

d e b a t e

b a l l o t

v o t i n g

Language Arts Words
Grammar

Name

Date

To parents
Starting on this page, your child will be introduced to reading and writing important words used in language arts. The pictures will help your child understand the meaning of each word.

■ Trace the letters while saying each word.

55

■ Trace the letters while saying each word.

singular

singular

singular

plural

plural

plural

prefix

prefix

prefix

suffix

suffix

suffix

Language Arts Words
Grammar

Name

Date

■ Trace the letters while saying each word.

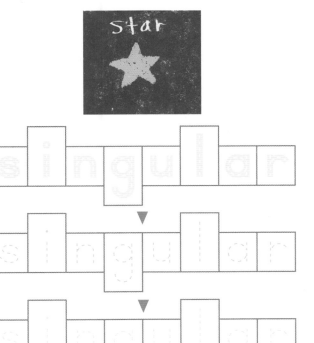

singular

singular

singular

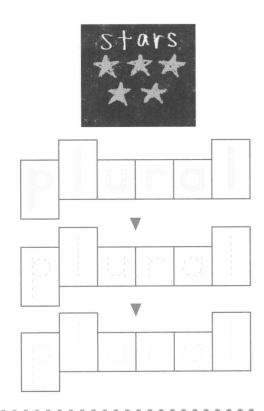

plural

plural

plural

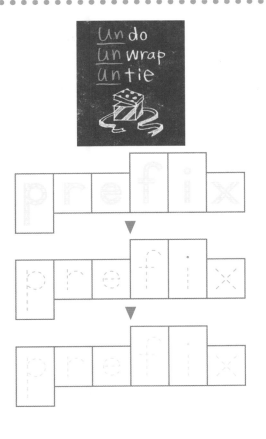

prefix

prefix

prefix

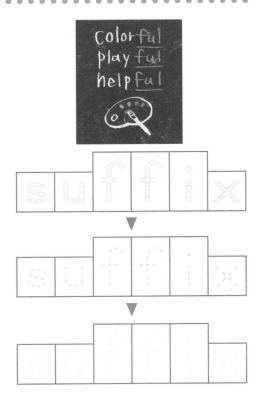

suffix

suffix

suffix

■ Trace and write the letters while saying each word.

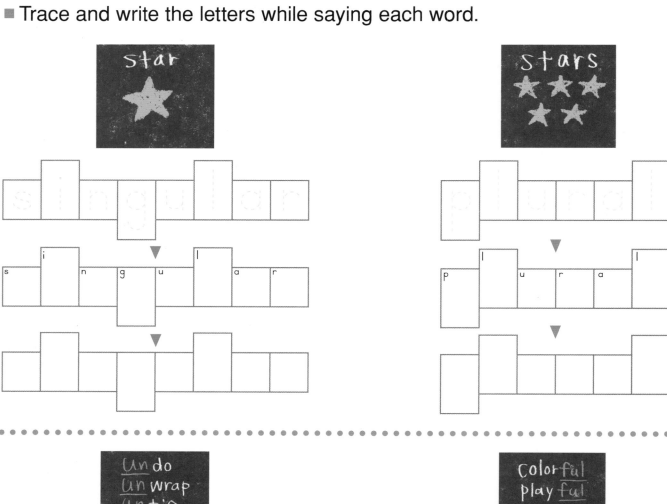

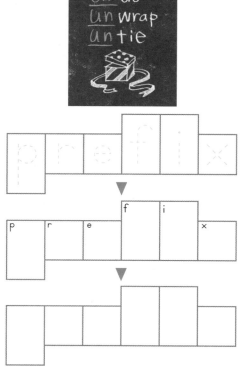

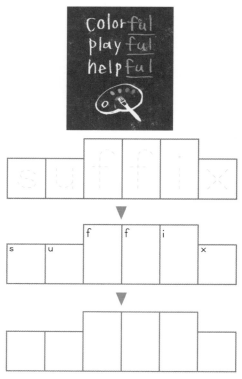

Language Arts Words
The Writing Process

Name

Date

■ Trace the letters while saying each word.

■ Trace the letters while saying each word.

planning

planning

planning

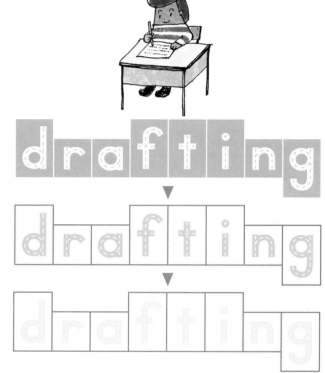

drafting

drafting

drafting

editing

editing

editing

sharing

sharing

sharing

31 Language Arts Words
The Writing Process

Name

Date

■ Trace the letters while saying each word.

planning
▼
planning
▼
planning

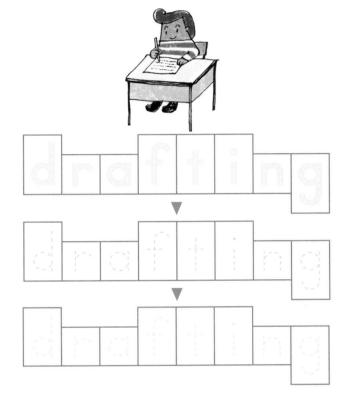

drafting
▼
drafting
▼
drafting

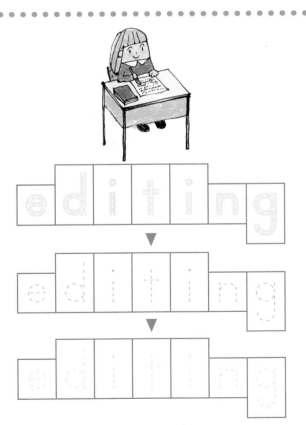

editing
▼
editing
▼
editing

sharing
▼
sharing
▼
sharing

61

■ Trace and write the letters while saying each word.

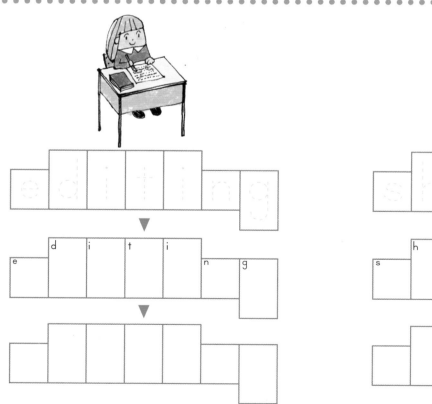

Name

Date

■ Write the letters while saying each word.

s i n g u l a r

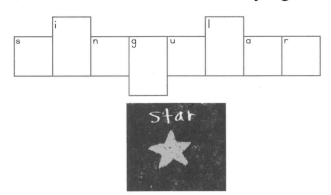

p l u r a l

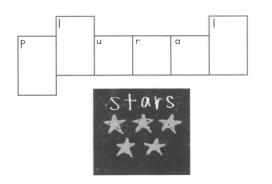

p r e f i x

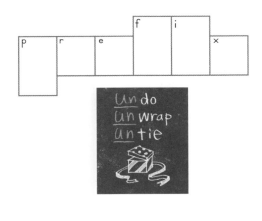

s u f f i x

p l a n n i n g

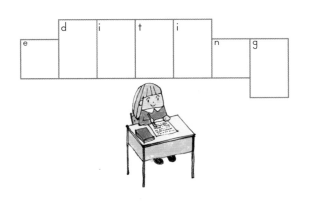

d r a f t i n g

e d i t i n g

s h a r i n g

To parents
This is the last page of this workbook before the final review. As an added challenge, the words on this page now appear in a mixed-up order. If your child has difficulty, help him or her focus on one word at a time.

■ Write the letters while saying each word.

Name

Date

■ Write the letters while saying each word.

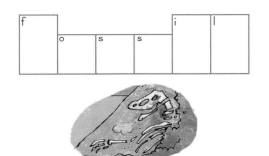

▶

···

f o s s i l

▶

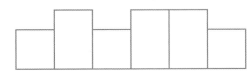

···

s h e l l s

▶

···

b o n e s

▶

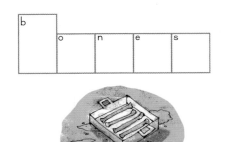

■ Write the letters while saying each word.

Name

Date

■ Write the letters while saying each word.

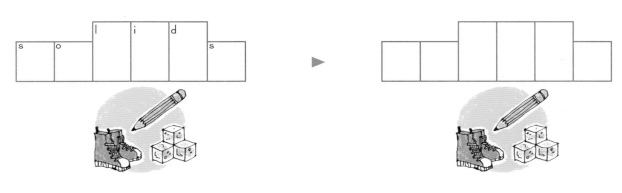

| s | o | l | i | d | s |

▶

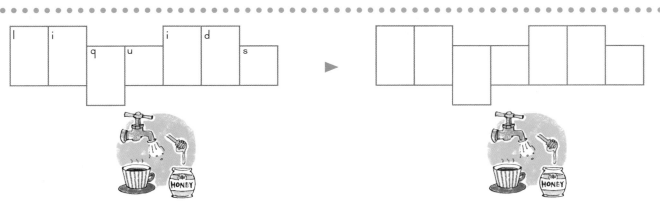

| l | i | q | u | i | d | s |

▶

| g | a | s | e | s |

▶

| m | a | t | t | e | r |

▶

■ Write the letters while saying each word.

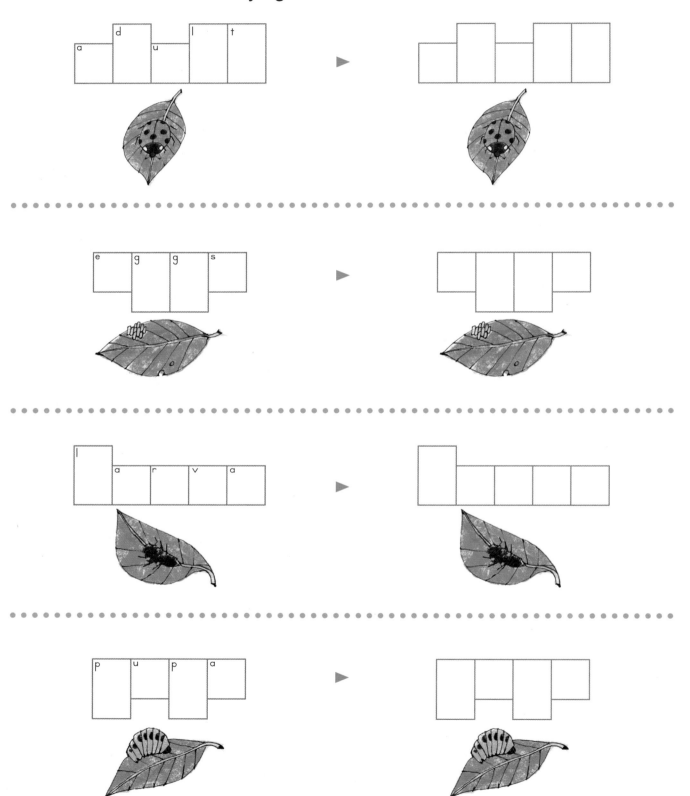

Name

Date

■ Write the letters while saying each word.

g	r	a	m

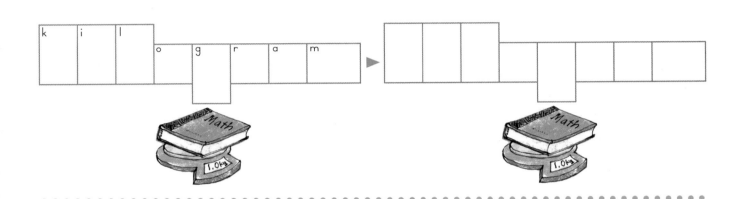

k	i	l

o	g	r	a	m

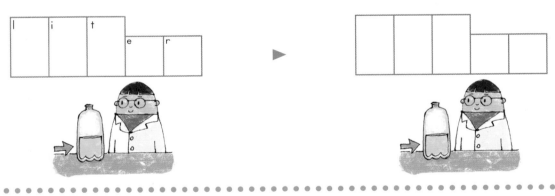

l	i	t

e	r

	t	
m	e	e	r

69

■ Write the letters while saying each word.

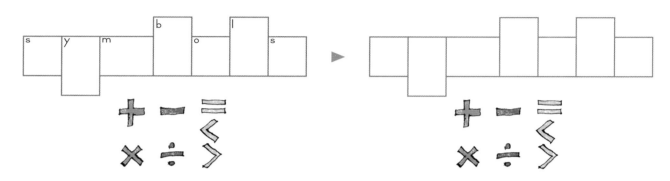

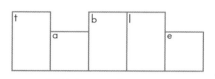 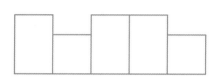

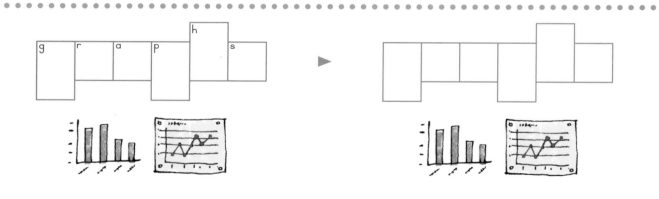

teacher	Number of students
Ms. Curley	23
Mr. Liu	21
Ms. Nunez	19
Mrs. Williams	22

teacher	Number of students
Ms. Curley	23
Mr. Liu	21
Ms. Nunez	19
Mrs. Williams	22

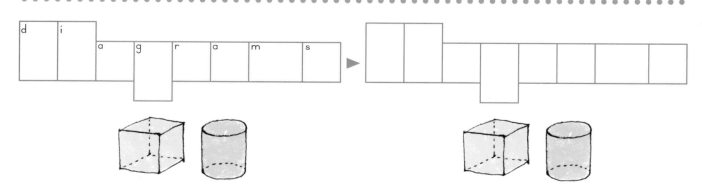

Name

Date

■ Write the letters while saying each word.

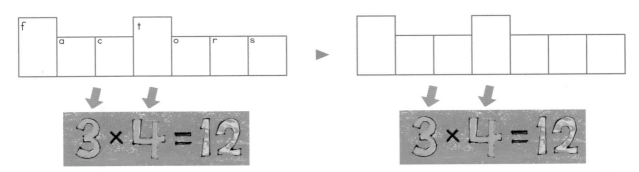

f a c t o r s

3 × 4 = 12

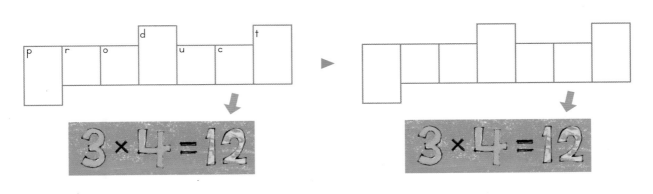

p r o d u c t

3 × 4 = 12

3 × 4 = 12

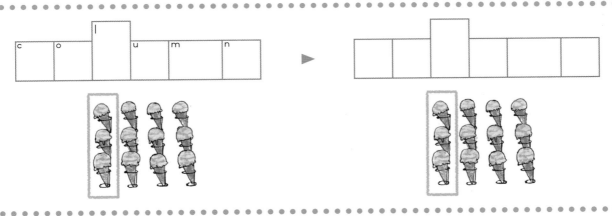

c o l u m n

r o w

■ Write the letters while saying each word.

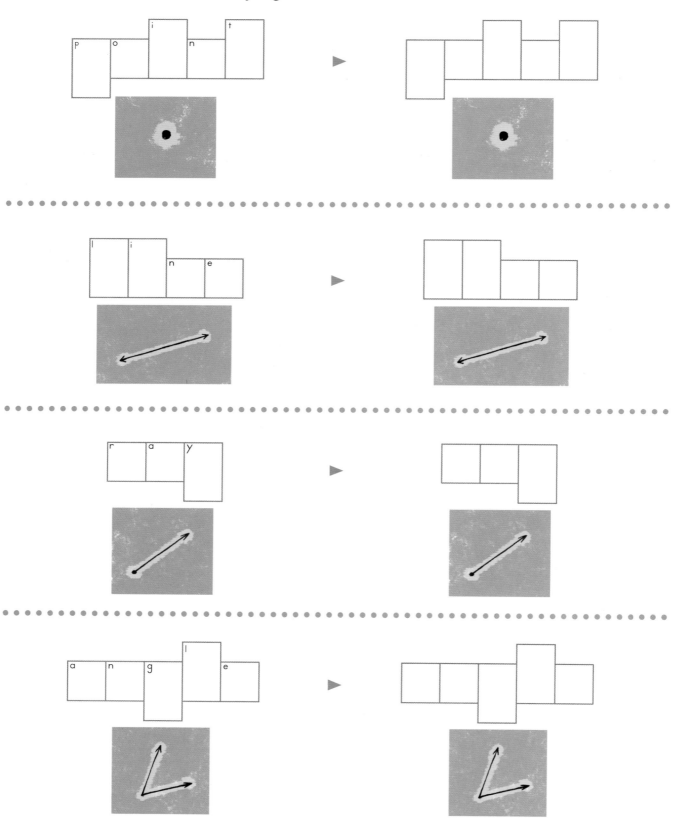

Review
Social Studies Words

Name

Date

■ Write the letters while saying each word.

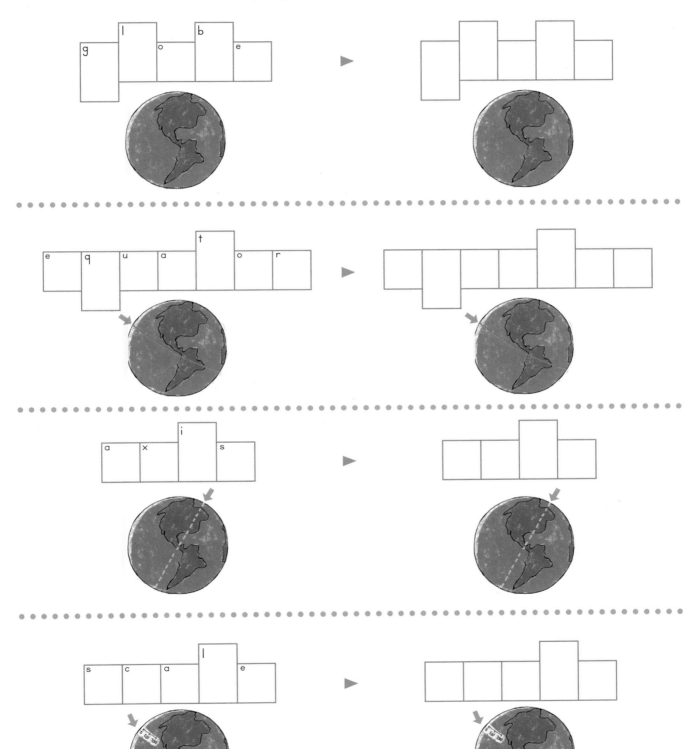

■ Write the letters while saying each word.

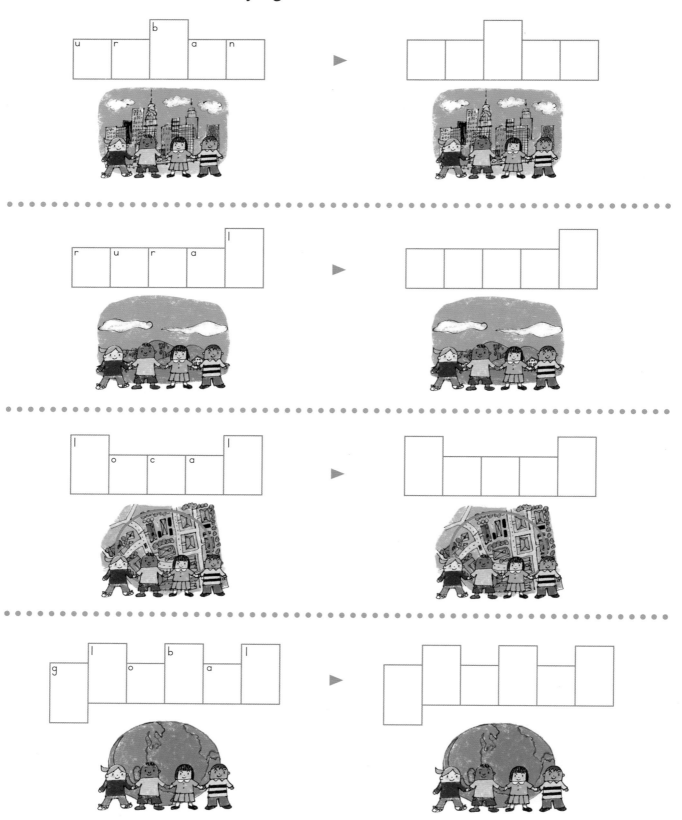

Review
Social Studies Words

■ Write the letters while saying each word.

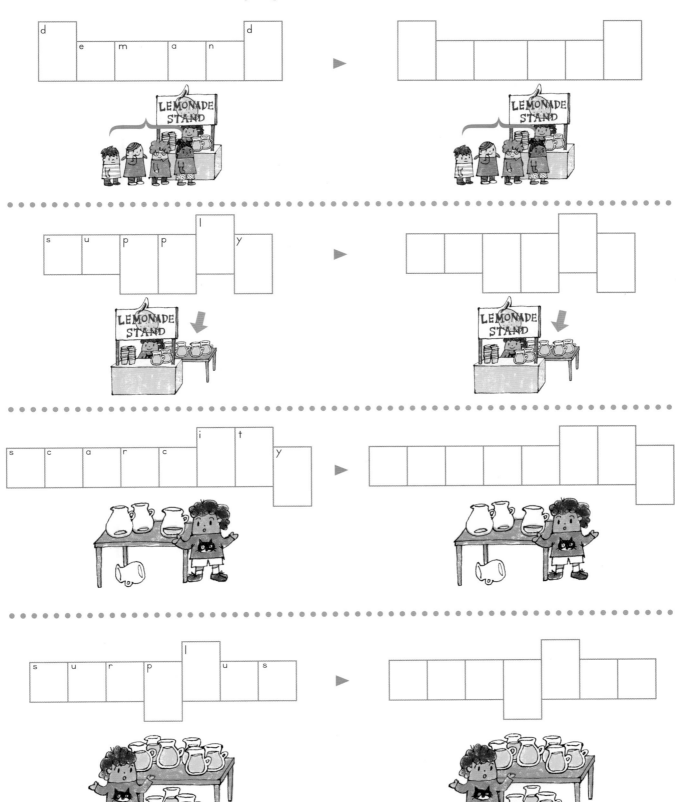

■ Write the letters while saying each word.

Name

Date

■ Write the letters while saying each word.

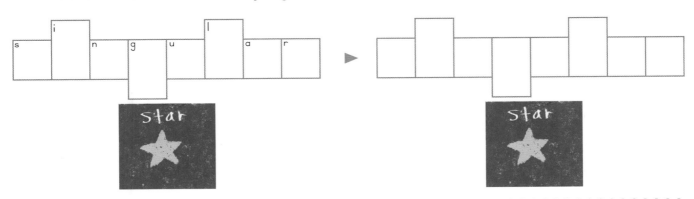

s | i | n | g | u | | l | a | r

star

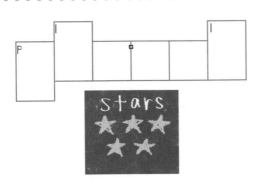

p | | l | | a | | | l

stars

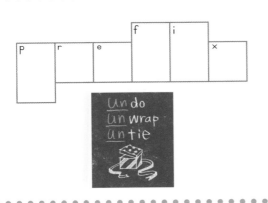

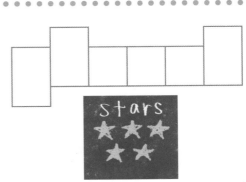

p | r | e | | f | i | | x

Undo
Unwrap
Untie

s | u | | f | f | i | | x

Colorful
playful
helpful

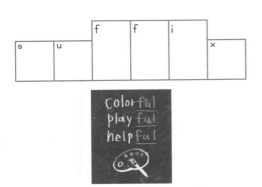

To parents
This is the last exercise of this workbook. Please praise
your child for the effort it took to complete this workbook.

Write the letters while saying each word.

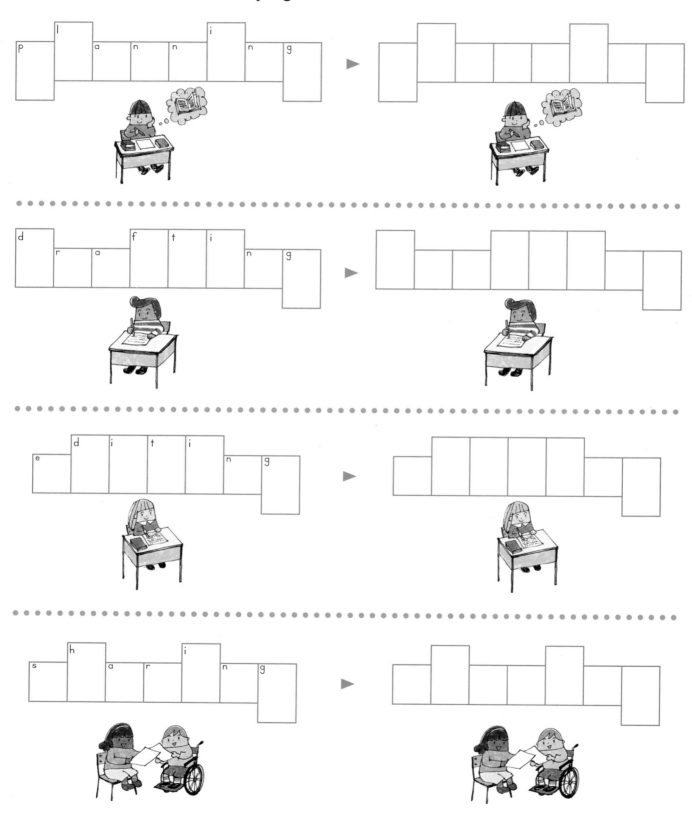

Certificate of Achievement

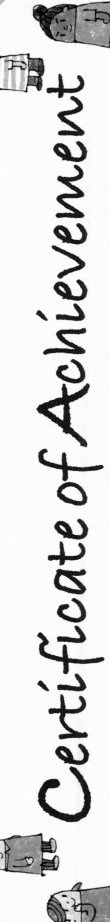

is hereby congratulated on completing

My Book of
WORDS FOR SCHOOL
LEVEL 4

Presented on

, 20

Parent or Guardian

KUM◯N